EAST LONDON

A 1960s Album

EAST LONDON

A 1960s Album

STEVE LEWIS

The
History
Press

First published as London's East End: A 1960s Album, 2010
This updated edition 2022

The History Press
97 St George's Place, Cheltenham,
Gloucestershire, GL50 3QB
www.thehistorypress.co.uk

British Library Cataloguing in Publication Data.
A catalogue record for this book is available from the British
Library.

ISBN 978 0 7509 9744 7

Typesetting and origination by The History Press
Printed and bound in Europe by Imak

CONTENTS

FOREWORD

All great cities around the world are defined by the areas that make them up – and in the case of London, can there be any other part as emblematic as the East End?

Go back to Roman times and you can see that even they identified that part of the city to locate their early settlements. In more recent times, from the Blitz of the Second World War to the boom times in banking in the late twentieth century, it was again at the epicentre.

But for acclaimed photographer Steve Lewis it was also his 'turf' – the home patch where he learnt his craft and honed the skills that were to take him to some of the most glamorous, and sometimes dangerous, places around the world during his lengthy career on a national newspaper.

As a photographer on a local paper in the East End, Steve was called on to cover everything from football to features and crime to glamour. For a man who has always sought to be creative with his work, and never just turn in a series of standard shots anyone else might be content with, it was to be the perfect blank canvas.

This compelling album shows a different side to today's East London and is from a time when it was a bustling but also gritty backdrop to families who had grown up there for generations, as well as the starting point for new arrivals to the country.

And if East London was from a different time, so was the whole country. Check out some of the fashions, hairstyles and cars and it seems like a weird and wonderful new planet! It's equally intriguing to see how, as you look through the album, Steve masters his craft and develops a style that was subsequently to propel him to work with some of the biggest names in British show business and in Hollywood too.

I was privileged to work with Steve for a number of years when I was on the showbiz beat for The Sun. Together we covered just about everything, from the impossible glamour of the making of a James Bond movie in a palace on an Indian lake, to the Cannes Film Festival, going on the road with Bruce Springsteen and even being caught up in the middle of a riot when the French police moved in.

But, just as London owes much of its roots to the East End so, too, does Steve, as this fascinating album will display.

Nick Ferrari, 2021
TV and radio presenter for LBC

INTRODUCTION

The photographs in this book capture the gritty reality of life in East London during the 'Swinging Sixties'. As the images graphically illustrate, the pop revolution and the advent of flower power had little discernible impact on the working-class Cockney.

East Enders were preoccupied with other concerns: widespread poverty, poor housing, industrial unrest, racial tension . . .

The area proved fertile ground for news-gatherers, among them Steve Lewis, destined to become a distinguished national newspaper photographer. In the 1960s, he covered Newham and surrounding boroughs for the local press and picture agencies. Equipped with a Nikon camera, he operated by the news desk mantra, 'Chase the story, get the faces.'

The following pages feature a selection of his assignments, ranging from neo-fascist intimidation of immigrants to the appalling squalor of 'halfway homes'.

On quiet days, Lewis focused on the disappearing vignettes of street life: the milkman straining under the weight of his Edwardian handcart; the rag-and-bone man plodding the streets with his horse-drawn waggon; the bicycle-borne totter with sign proclaiming, 'Complete Homes Purchased'.

Many of the locations in which Lewis worked have changed beyond recognition. Tower blocks supplanted swathes of Blitz-scarred terraces; the Docklands were recast as the capital's alternative commercial hub. Now the site of the 2012 Olympics offers new vistas.

As the old fabric of the East End was consigned to memory, so were many of its traditions. Here is a unique glimpse of the way it was . . .

Geoff Compton

legacy of war

Two decades on, the scars of the Blitz still disfigured swathes of the East End. In this vista from a new tower block, rubble-strewn gaps in the terraces mark the random pattern of the aerial onslaught. Half-a-dozen homes have vanished from the street immediately below. To the right, an entire row has been razed.

Widespread redevelopment regularly led to discoveries of unexploded wartime bombs, requiring the delicate skills and limitless courage of UXB teams. Two army bomb disposal experts defuse a 2,000lb bomb unearthed close to the busy East Ham–Barking bypass. The chain-smoking officer laconically told photographer Steve Lewis, 'Don't worry. If it starts ticking, you'll have a full six seconds to leg it.'

a nation at work

Unemployment fell to an all-time low in the mid-Sixties as the economy began to surge. With new-tech in its infancy, most men were still engaged in manual work. Weekly wages averaging £20 were paid in cash. Women's pay lagged far behind but surveys reflected a public mood of optimism for the future. Britain was back in business.

life in the slow lane

A sixpenny bus ride away in Kings Road and Carnaby Street, the sixties were swinging fit to burst. Here, life followed less frenetic rhythms, and fashion trends extended only to a mandatory hat. On these and following pages, Steve Lewis captures the flavour of East London life in the slower lane.

home sweet home

Nissen huts were built in the 1940s as temporary accommodation for families left homeless by German bombing. These in Bridge Road, Stratford, were still occupied in 1969. The corrugated-asbestos makeshifts, constructed by Italian prisoners of war, were difficult to heat in winter and stifling in summer. Yet the residents were not clamouring to be rehoused.

'I've been here since 1945 and I've become attached to the place,' said Mrs Elsie Osborne. 'After all, a home is only what you make it.' Her neighbour, hirsute artist Charles Mears (seen on p. 15) echoed her sentiments. 'I'm quite happy living here, just as long as I'm left in peace to get on with my paintings.'

Newham Council, however, planned to redevelop the site 'within the next few years'.

trapped indoors

An alarming number of Newham's elderly and disabled were confined to their homes because of an acute shortage of wheelchairs. The borough's Public Health Department had 120, all out on loan, and there was urgent need for as many again. After a long delay, Stratford pensioner Daisy Rook (pictured) took delivery of a council wheelchair – only to find that its wheelbase was too wide for the narrow front door of her second-floor flat. 'We've asked them to change it for something suitable,' said a neighbour. 'Daisy last left her flat more than a year ago, and that was for an ambulance trip to hospital. She can't wait to be taken to the shops and the park.' The council was appealing for public donations of wheelchairs, regardless of their condition.

long live the duke

An unsettling wind of change was ruffling feathers in many of Newham's 176 drinking haunts. The Spotted Dog in Forest Gate, one of the East End's oldest pubs, had been transformed into a steakhouse, and scores of others were undergoing makeovers in a bid to cash in on the Swinging Sixties.

However, it was business as usual down at the Duke of Fife in Katherine Road, Forest Gate. To the relief of his mainly grey-haired regulars, 'guv'nor' Alf Hales had vowed, 'There'll be no change here. We're a traditional pub and we're not catering for youngsters.' He had the full support of lifelong customers Rose Walsham (left) and Susan Lawrence. 'I wouldn't come here again if they started mucking the place about,' said Rose, aged 73. Her tippling chum Susan, 77, was equally hostile to the juke-box trend. 'My mother first brought me here in my pram,' she recalled, over a pint of stout. 'The pub is home to me and I couldn't bear it to change. We have a good old sing-song at weekends. Come here on a Saturday night and you'll see me giving a turn.'

The cloth-capped gents in the public bar were too engrossed in their card game to comment. It seems safe to assume that they liked things just the way they were.

feeding the fans

'Peanuts, luvverly peanuts!' No outing to a football match would be the same
without them (the nuts still in their shells, of course). Here, a street vendor does
a roaring trade at the gates of West Ham United Football Club in 1965.

interlude

'What is this life if, full of care,
We have no time to stand and stare . . .'
W.H. Davies

maternal instincts

With no shortage of role models to imitate, these pram-pushing youngsters
with their dolls get into motherhood mode . . . not a sight to gladden hearts
in the women's liberation movement.

working mum

Mini-skirted Lesley Lucking combined the roles of Lollipop Lady and doting mother, shepherding schoolchildren across the pedestrian crossing – while never being more than a heartbeat away from her baby daughter Tracey, sleeping soundly in the pram at the kerbside.

four-legged friends

Horse power was still an essential component of 1960s street commerce, a fact celebrated in television's then-new comedy hit *Steptoe and Son*. By and large, East Enders had a sentimental regard for these beasts of burden, John Loftus being a case in point. John, licensee of the Manby Arms in Stratford, acquired retired donkey 'Bass' a few weeks before, and customers soon became accustomed to the animal supping ale alongside them in the public bar.

gift of the gab

Their motto was, 'Pile it high, sell
it cheap'. Whether the barrow was
laden with cockles and whelks
or apples and pears, the Cockney
costermonger was as much showman
as market trader. Success depended
on developing the vocal chords of a
drill sergeant-major, plus a quickfire
line in cheeky patter to make the
ladies laugh.

weekend workers

In an age when kids' pocket money was scarce, these
youngsters were only too willing to earn a few bob helping out
with Saturday morning deliveries.

big ideas

The sign proclaims 'COMPLETE Homes Purchased', suggesting a Herculean effort by this elderly entrepreneur and his removal transport.

pushing pintas

The hernia-threatening mode of transport may be outmoded but milkman Alfred Davies was firmly wedded to his Edwardian handcart. Alfred, who had been delivering pints to Forest Gate doorsteps for more than thirty years, explained, 'The round keeps me feeling young. There's no better way to keep fit and the barrow never breaks down – not like those electric milk floats.'

last-chance saloon

Visit the Beckton Marshes any night of the week and you would find a dozen or
more vagrant alcoholics gathered in a cluster of foul-smelling concrete shelters
close to the Royal Albert Dock. For many, this was the final stop before the
cemetery. Walter (p. 41 top left) was typical. After fighting with the Argylls in Korea,
he left the army, failed to find steady work and became an alcoholic. He drank
methylated spirits, otherwise known as 'jake'. When the meths ran out, he melted
shoe polish and drank that. Walter was dying and he knew it. His liver was all but
destroyed, and severe malnutrition would do the rest. Volunteers from the Simon
Community charity, who estimated there were around 500 'jakies' in Newham,
visited the men nightly, persuading some to move to their East End refuge.
'We run the place on a tier system,' explained organiser Jim Horne. 'On the ground
floor, they live and drink. If they want to come off the stuff, they move upstairs
to the "dry" room. A few stay up for three months or more but almost all of them
go back downstairs eventually.' He continued, 'Then, more often than not, they
headed back to the marshes. . . '

sweet dreams

Oblivious to the din of passing traffic in Mile End Road, Aldgate, this weary gentleman of the road takes advantage of a vacant bench to sleep off a heavy – possibly liquid – lunch.

man for all seasons

This urban beachcomber, apparently immune to the elements, was a familiar
figure on the streets of Whitechapel and Stepney. Stripped to the waist,
summer and winter, he spent his days collecting wire and old newspapers.

making do

'The kids have nothing to do round here.' That's the time-worn complaint of parents throughout the area. As ever, youngsters created their own diversions, wasteland and derelict cars proving an irresistible magnet.

playmates

Racial harmony might seem only a distant possibility in the adult world, but these young East Enders made no distinctions in their choice of playmates.

messsages of hate

The Race Relations Act of 1965, outlawing discrimination in public places, failed to stem the tide of intolerance and intimidation in inner city areas. Three years later, an inflammatory speech by senior Tory Enoch Powell raised tensions to new heights. Powell forecast 'rivers of blood' unless immigration was halted. Black newcomers were now subjected to racial taunts on a regular basis at work and in the streets. Clashes between neo-fascist and far-left groups mirrored the graffiti war being fought on walls across the East End. In Whitechapel, a group of National Front supporters came by night to nail their message of hate to the front door of a West Indian family.

make love not war

The slogan-writers have been busy. Racism and anti-racism apart, the messages reflect
the main preoccupations of the day. Top of the list are the Vietnam War and trade union
militancy. And sex, of course.

halfway to hell

Eight adults and fifteen children crammed into a single terraced house which is in urgent need of repair. Two toilets, one bathroom, one kitchen, shared by all. These are the statistics of misery at a typical 'halfway home'. Officially, these council-run properties provided short-term refuge for the homeless. Too often, families found themselves trapped in this twilight zone for years. Newham councillor Jim Hucker was calling for the wholesale closure of the authority's homes.

'They must be shut down on humanitarian grounds,' he declared. 'Nobody should be asked to live like animals. I know many of these people are there because they owe rent but that is no reason to kick them in the teeth like this.'

The uncomfortable truth is that many 'conventional' council tenants endured conditions that were little better. The images here and on the following pages highlight the grim plight of thousands in Newham and surrounding boroughs.

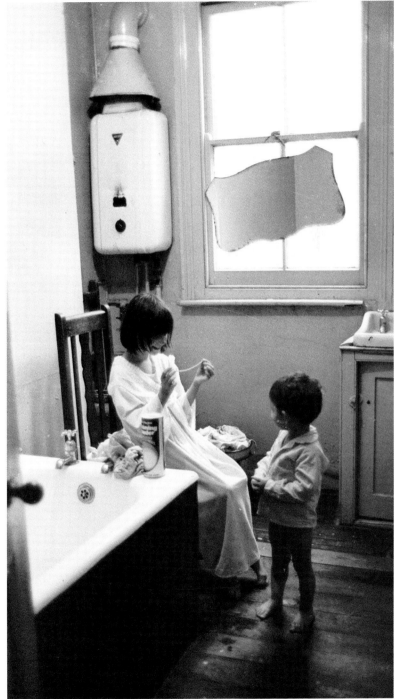

old habits

A spacious flat in one of the new tower blocks may have been a huge improvement on two rooms and outside loo in a Victorian terrace, but residents complained of feeling isolated in their high-rise homes. As a throwback to a convivial chat over the backyard wall, these young mothers congregated for a chinwag on a nearby bombsite each morning.

It was also an ideal spot for exercising the pet sheep.

positive results

Under the stern gaze of two policemen, a driver undergoes a breath test in 1968 following a backstreet collision. It had been just over a year since the introduction of the breathalyser, and official figures showed that road traffic accidents involving alcohol had decreased from 25 per cent to 15 per cent. When the 1967 Road Safety Act first imposed a limit on motorists' drink consumption, licensed victuallers protested that they would be put out of business. However, in reality the crackdown had little effect on takings at the traditional East End pub.

forever blowing bubbles

Unless West Ham United's performance improved dramatically before the end of the 1969/70 season, it would be a year the players would rather forget. However, the string of poor results had done nothing to dampen support on the terraces. For these young fans, the Upton Park fixtures were still the biggest thrill that half-a-crown could buy. They were pinning their hopes on the club's new signing, legendary striker Jimmy Greaves, pictured overleaf with team-mate and World Cup hero Geoff Hurst, to start hammering in those much-needed goals.

colourful past

The centuries-old Two Puddings in Stratford Broadway became rather gentrified, a venue for family Sunday lunches. Once upon a time, it was very different, an establishment oft-visited by the boys in blue when they were looking for likely lads. That colourful East End double act, the Kray twins, for example, were known to have made their mark here on more than one occasion.

the people's palace

The arc lights would soon be switched on, and the spectacle would begin – greyhounds rocketing around the track, the crowd roaring deliriously, waiters dispensing booze and chicken-in-a-basket. To experience East Londoners having a good night out, Walthamstow Stadium was the place to be. The bookmakers would, of course, play a leading role in the show – helping punters to part with their hard-earned cash. In the lull before curtain-up, the men in black suits fortify themselves with steaming cuppas.

snapper snapped

David Bailey, one of the world's
leading fashion photographers,
found himself on the other side
of the lens when fellow East
Ender Steve Lewis dropped in
on him. Bailey, pictured with
American girlfriend Penelope
Tree, was preparing to fly to
India on a five-week assignment
for *Vogue* magazine – a quantum
leap from his schoolboy
experiments with a box Brownie
camera. His mother Mrs Gladys
Bailey, who still prepared Sunday
lunches for him at the family
home in Heigham Road, East
Ham, remained unimpressed by
her son's celebrity status.
'She thinks my lifestyle is mad,'
said Bailey. 'She would much
rather I'd been a nice, happily
married bank clerk. But I just
wasn't clever enough for that.'

style shock

Shockwaves from the style explosion centred on Carnaby Street were beginning to ripple out to the East End. Stratford was the unlikely venue for this mid-1960s fashion shoot which, quite literally, stopped the traffic. A large crowd gathered to gawp at the girls strutting their stuff in luridly hued ensembles featuring must-have hot pants.

Another, equally eye-catching fashion statement was being made just a mile away, proving that the Cockney tradition of Pearly Kings and Queens was alive and well. These families preparing for Harvest Festival, their flagship event, were carrying on a tradition begun in 1875. That's when young Londoner Henry Croft had the brainwave of plastering his clothes with pearl buttons, a gimmick that helped him stand out in the crowd and promote his crusade to raise money for the needy. Today's Pearlies, the 'aristocracy' of market traders, continue the charity work.

winning smiles

Beauty contests were a rite of passage for teenage girls dreaming of becoming the next Twiggy or Jean Shrimpton. The shows were a staple of British life; towns across the country crowned a new 'queen' annually. These ladies may not have graduated to the cover of *Vogue*, but their smiles certainly enhanced the pages of the *Newham Recorder*

woes on wheels

No strangers to persecution, the Romany community in East London faced varying levels of hostility. The untidy campsites dotted around the boroughs were widely regarded as a blot on the landscape. They had become flashpoints for local hostility and represented a recurring headache for police and local authorities. The issue got lurid coverage in the many weekly newspapers.

A typical headline, 'GIPSY SHOWDOWN FEARS', appeared above a report of the town clerk's warning that forcible clearance of a site near Rathbone Market, Canning Town, may trigger 'a pitched battle'. In 1969 Newham Council voted to provide temporary facilities at a large encampment close to the East Ham–Barking Bypass, giving the travellers a five-year reprieve.

'This is great news,' said caravan-dweller Mrs Mary Riley, a mother of four (pictured, peeling potatoes). 'We've been here three months and we like the place. There's a lot of rubbish around but when that's cleared up the site will be all right.'

Her enthusiasm was not shared by all. Ratepayer councillor Mike Talbot said, 'This is one of the worst decisions ever taken by the council.'

Here and on the following pages, is a portrait of the travellers' precarious existence.

troubled waters

This deceptively tranquil waterfront scene gives no hint of the turbulence that rendered the East London Docklands the epicentre of union militancy in Britain. The 1960s saw labour relations hit a new low, with 'work-to-rule' and strikes frequently threatening to bring the Port of London to a complete standstill. The issues were wages and, crucially, working practices. The docks had been in steady decline since the Second World War, and both government and bosses were demanding root-and-branch modernisation. The dock workers, led by the TGWU's charismatic firebrand Jack Dash, were fighting an increasingly bitter battle to preserve jobs, boost pay and control working procedures. The docks, once the commercial crossroads of an empire, were now in their death throes.

ACKNOWLEDGEMENTS

To the *Newham Recorder* for giving me the freedom to express myself with my camera.

To Tom Duncan, the editor of the paper, who had the foresight to see the changes that were happening in the East End.

To journalist Terry Chinery with whom I worked on many of the stories that appeared in the paper.

To my close friend Geoff Compton who was then news editor of the *Newham Recorder* and helped me research the book and with his remarkable memory has written the words to go with my photographs.

I would like to thank Jenni Munro-Collins at Newham Heritage & Archives for her help in tracing the locations and dating some of the photographs.

And to the people of the East End for allowing me to take their pictures.

Steve Lewis can be contacted at www.stevelewisphotography.com and is represented by Getty Images www.gettyimages.co.uk